D1518989

Explore and Draw

SHARKS

DRAWING AND READING

Gare Thompson

ROURKE PUBLISHING

www.rourkepublishing.com

Editor: Penny Dowdy
Art Direction: Cheena Yadav (Q2AMedia)
Designer: Suzena Samuel, Jasmeen Kaur (Q2AMedia)
Illustrator: Vinay Kumar Sharma
Picture researcher: Rajeev Parmar (Q2AMedia)

Picture credits:
t=top b=bottom c=centre l=left r=right
Cover: Roessler Carl/Photolibrary
Back Cover: BackRod Kaye/Istockphoto, Roessler Carl/Photolibrary, Cretolamna/Shutterstock, Nathan Jones/Istockphoto, David Lewis/Istockphoto, Tischenko Irina/Shutterstock, Malou Leontsinis/Shutterstock, Radoslav Stoilov/Shutterstock, Close Encounters Photography/Shutterstock, CTR Photos/Shutterstock.
Title page: Pnicoledolin/Shutterstock, Ian Scott/Shutterstock, Cbpix/Shutterstock, Fiona Ayerst/Shutterstock, Philip Lange/Shutterstock, Fiona Ayerst/Shutterstock.
Insides: Pnicoledolin/Shutterstock, Ian Scott/Shutterstock, Cbpix/Shutterstock, Fiona Ayerst/Shutterstock, Philip Lange/Shutterstock, Fiona Ayerst/Shutterstock. Pnicoledolin/Shutterstock, Ian Scott/Shutterstock, Cbpix/Shutterstock, Fiona Ayerst/Shutterstock, Philip Lange/Shutterstock, Fiona Ayerst/Shutterstock: 4- 24, A Cotton Photo/Shutterstock: 6, Chuck Babbitt/Istockphoto: 7,
Chris and Monique Fallows/Photolibrary: 10, Fiona Ayerst /Shutterstock: 11, Soury /Photolibrary: 14, Chris Newbert/Minden Pictures/FLPA: 15, Fred Bavendam/Minden Pictures/FLPA: 18.

Q2AMedia Image Bank: 19.
Q2AMedia Art Bank: Cover, Title Page, 4-5, 8-9, 12-13, 16-17, 20-21, Back Cover.

Library of Congress Cataloging-in-Publication Data

Becker, Ann, 1965 Oct. 6-
Sharks: explore and draw / Gare Thompson.
p. cm. – (Explore and draw)
Includes index.
ISBN 978-1-61590-252-1 (hard cover)
ISBN 978-1-61590-492-1 (soft cover)
1.Sharks in art–Juvenile literature. 2. Drawing–Technique–Juvenile literature.
I. Title. II. Title: Explore and draw.
NC825.A4B43 2009
743'.8962913334–dc22
2009021617

Rourke Publishing
Printed in the United States of America, North Mankato, Minnesota
033010
033010LP

www.rourkepublishing.com - rourke@rourkepublishing.com
Post Office Box 643328 Vero Beach, Florida 32964

Contents

Technique

Are you ready to draw sharks? First, you need to understand the basic form of a shark. There are certain shapes you can use to sketch the shark. Using a midline will help. The midline works as the center of the shark's body.

1

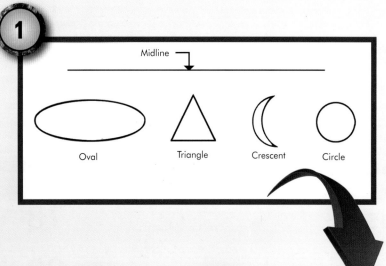

Ovals, triangles, crescents, and circles are the basic shapes used to draw sharks. Observe the **proportions** of a shark. Use the midline to help draw the shapes in the correct position.

Sharks' bodies have an oval shape. Draw an oval around a midline. Then, add a crescent shape to the end of the midline for the shark's tail.

2

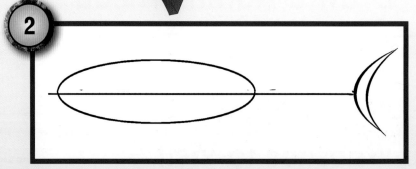

3 Draw a circle for the shark's eye. Add triangles for the fins and the **snout**. Draw a crescent for the tail.

4 Lightly draw guidelines to connect the shapes. This forms the framework of the shark. Erase any extra lines.

5 Use light and dark tones to **shade** the shapes. This gives the shark **dimension**. This will make your drawing more interesting.

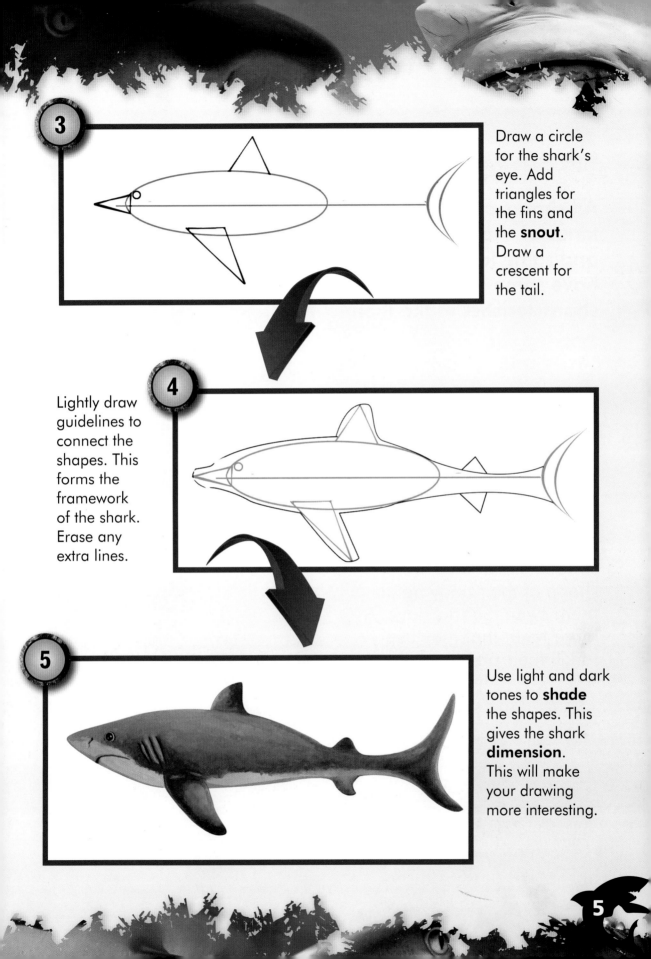

Meet the Sharks

All sharks are fish, but there are different kinds of sharks. Some sharks are scary and some look odd. Most sharks, however, have some common characteristics. Their characteristics make them special.

The Shark Body

Unlike most fish, sharks do not have bones. Their **skeleton** is made up of **cartilage**. Cartilage is light and flexible. Sharks have smooth, sleek bodies shaped like a torpedo. The shape of their body helps them swim. Sharks have large teeth that they use to kill their **prey**.

A group of sharks attacking prey is called a feeding frenzy.

When sharks lose teeth, new teeth grow in. Some sharks replace over 30,000 teeth in their lifetime.

Swift Swimmers

The shark's fins help it swim. Its stiff side fins push its body forward, acting like underwater wings or propellers. The large fin on the shark's back keeps it from rolling over. The shark also uses its fins to help it turn. The shark swims all the time. It would sink and die if it stopped.

Shark Senses

Sharks' super senses make them different from other fish. They have sharp eyes, keen hearing, and a powerful sense of smell. These senses help sharks when they hunt for prey. Sharks also have other senses. They can feel vibrations or movement in the water. This helps keep sharks safe from **predators**. Sharks can also feel electric **impulses** from their prey. This helps them hunt.

Draw a Shark

Sharks' bodies are sleek and smooth. This helps them swim. They use their tail and fins to move swiftly through the water.

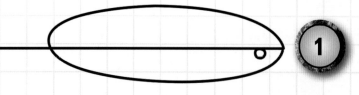

1 Draw a midline. Draw an oval around it. Add a small circle for the eye.

2 Draw a triangle at the top of the oval for a dorsal fin. Add a crescent behind the oval for a tail fin. Connect the body to the tail with two curved guidelines. Then, draw a small triangle at the front of the oval for the snout.

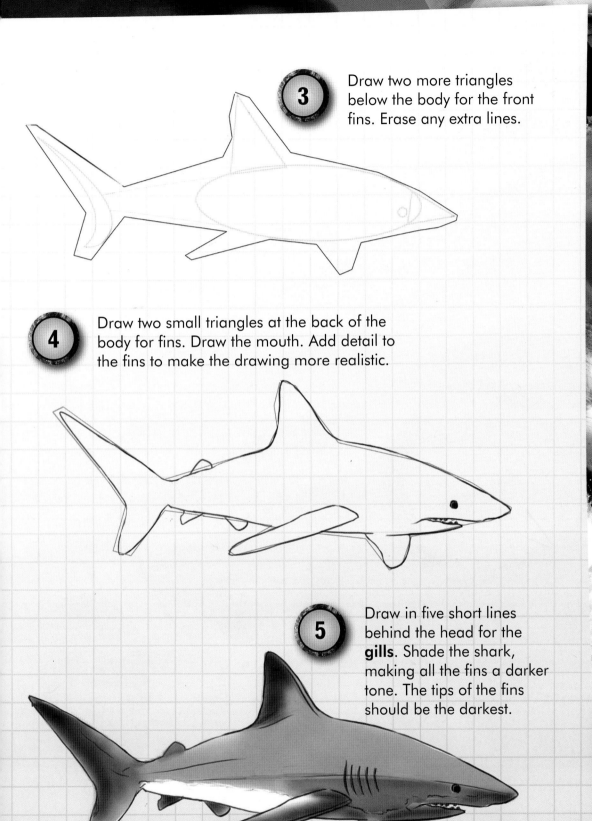

3 Draw two more triangles below the body for the front fins. Erase any extra lines.

4 Draw two small triangles at the back of the body for fins. Draw the mouth. Add detail to the fins to make the drawing more realistic.

5 Draw in five short lines behind the head for the **gills**. Shade the shark, making all the fins a darker tone. The tips of the fins should be the darkest.

Scary Sharks

Most people are afraid of sharks. Here are three scary sharks that live in oceans.

The Great White Shark

The great white shark is the largest **carnivore**, or meat-eating, shark. It grows to about 13-17 feet (4-5.2 meters) long and weighs up to 2,400 pounds (1,100 kilograms). This shark is also called white death. It is one big, scary fish! Even though its main food is seals, this shark scares people!

Great white sharks sometimes mistake humans in the water for seals. That is why they attack people.

The Tiger Shark

Young tiger sharks have stripes like a tiger, but the stripes fade as the tiger sharks get older. Tiger sharks can grow to be 13.9 feet (4.25 meters) long and weigh up to 1,400 pounds (635 kilograms). These sharks hunt mostly at night. Tiger sharks eat almost anything, including other sharks. Their sharp teeth and strong jaws make them deadly predators.

The Bull Shark

Bull sharks live in the ocean. Unlike other sharks, they sometimes swim up rivers. Finding these sharks in rivers make many people think bull sharks are the scariest sharks. Bull sharks are only 10 feet (3 meters) long, but they can attack hippos. Like tiger sharks, bull sharks eat almost anything. Bull sharks get their name from their short, blunt snout.

Bull sharks use their snout like bulls when they headbutt their prey.

Draw a Great White Shark

Great white sharks' bodies are shaped like torpedoes. Their powerful tail helps move them through the water. Great white sharks have about 3,000 teeth. That's one reason they are so scary.

1 Draw a midline. Draw an oval around it. Add a small circle for the eye.

2 Add a crescent for the tail. Draw a triangle at the top of the oval for a dorsal fin. Next, draw a smaller triangle for the snout. Then, add smaller triangles near the tail for the back fins.

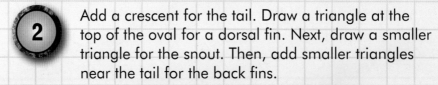

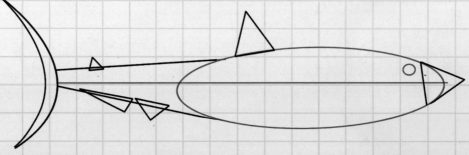

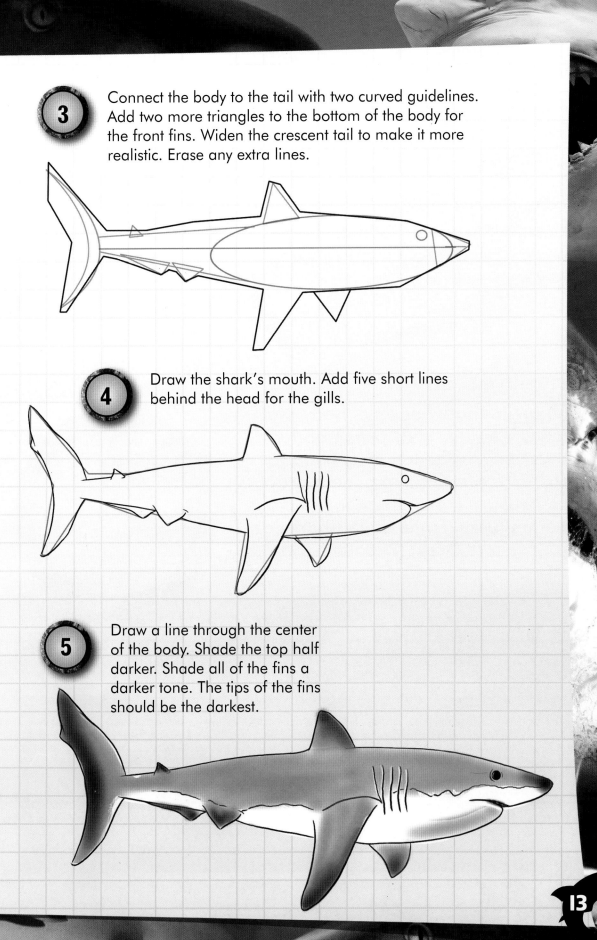

3 Connect the body to the tail with two curved guidelines. Add two more triangles to the bottom of the body for the front fins. Widen the crescent tail to make it more realistic. Erase any extra lines.

4 Draw the shark's mouth. Add five short lines behind the head for the gills.

5 Draw a line through the center of the body. Shade the top half darker. Shade all of the fins a darker tone. The tips of the fins should be the darkest.

Odd Sharks

Some sharks look very odd, having strange shapes or colors. These sharks use **camouflage** to keep safe and to hunt.

The Angel Shark

The angel shark has a flat body that blends into the sandy ocean bottom. It has eyes on the top of its head to search for prey. Its sharp teeth are like needles. It uses them to eat crabs and **mollusks**. Some angel sharks can grow up to 6.5 feet (2 meters) long.

The angel shark's long, wide fins look like wings.

Wobbegongs

A wobbegong is small. It only grows to 4.1 feet (1.25 meters), but it is tricky. The wobbegong looks like seaweed as it waits for shrimp and fish to swim by. Then its mouth opens, and it eats its prey. Since it looks so much like seaweed, people in Japan sometimes step on it. Guess what happens? Right, the wobbegong will take a bite out of a person's foot!

The Swell Shark

Unlike the wobbegong and the angel shark, the swell shark uses camouflage to keep safe. This shark is often blotchy brown and small. It only grows to about 3.94 feet (1.2 meters). Its color and size help it hide from predators. Often it hides in **crevices**, or small cracks, in the ocean floor. It can then swell up and fill the crack, safely hiding from its enemies.

Some wobbegongs have tassels around their mouth that float in the water like seaweed.

Draw a Wobbegong

Wobbegongs have flat bodies and heads. They have fringe around their head. Their fringe looks like seaweed or whiskers. Wobbegongs hide and wait for their prey.

1 Draw a curved midline. Draw an oval around it. Add a small circle for the eye.

2 Draw a long triangle at the back end for the tail. Add small triangles to the top and bottom of the tail for the back fins. Draw two larger triangles toward the front of the shark for the front fins. Add a crescent at the front for the snout.

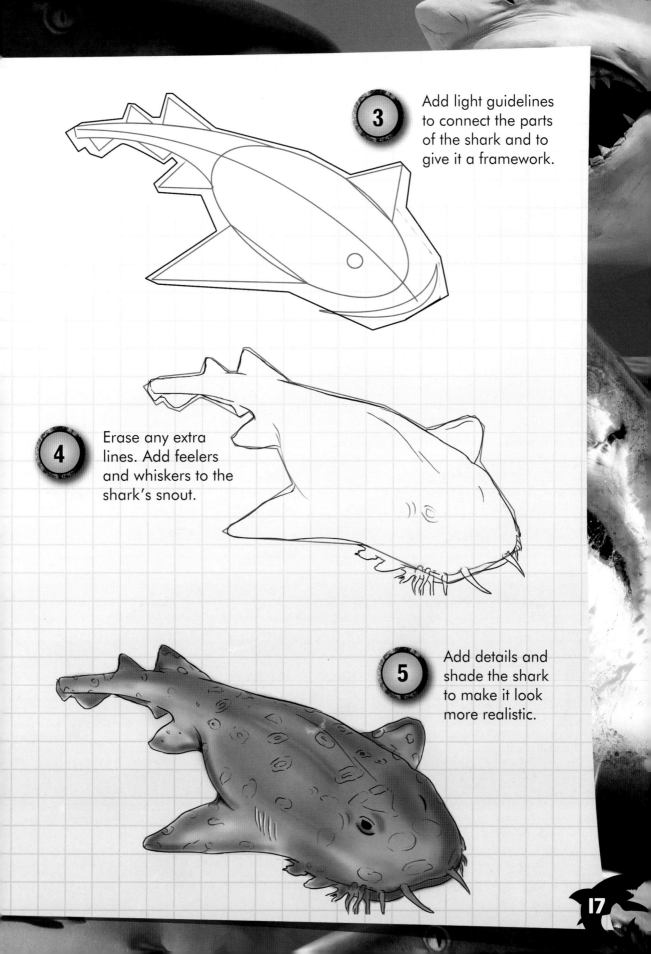

3 Add light guidelines to connect the parts of the shark and to give it a framework.

4 Erase any extra lines. Add feelers and whiskers to the shark's snout.

5 Add details and shade the shark to make it look more realistic.

Hammerheads

Most people know hammerhead sharks. They are easy to spot because their wide, flat head looks like a hammer!

The Scalloped Hammerhead

The most common hammerhead shark is the scalloped hammerhead. Its head is curved at the front, making it look like a scallop. These sharks grow to be about 13.2 feet (4 meters) long. These odd-looking sharks live in tropical regions. Normally they eat small fish, such as sardines, but they can eat octopus, too. They live in large **schools**, or groups.

Hundreds of scalloped hammerheads can belong to one school.

The great hammerhead often eats the dangerous stingray. The stinging needles stay in the shark's jaw.

The Great Hammerhead

The great hammerhead is the biggest and scariest of the hammerhead sharks. It can grow to 20 feet (6.1 meters) and weigh about 500 pounds (230 kilograms). The great hammerhead is an active hunter. It eats mainly bony prey, such as lobsters and catfish. It hunts at dusk along the seafloor. Living in warm regions, this large, frightening shark has attacked people.

The Shovelhead

The shovelhead is the smallest and most harmless of the hammerheads. This shark, also called the bonnethead, only grows to about 3.3 feet (1 meter). It has both sharp and broad, flat teeth so it can eat both hard and soft sea creatures. Unlike the scalloped hammerhead, it swims in schools of only five to fifteen fish.

Draw a Hammerhead

Hammerheads have heads that look like hammers. Their eyes are at the side of their heads. This helps them see their prey. Hammerheads are great hunters.

1 Draw a curved midline. Draw an oval around it.

2 Draw a small crescent at the rear of the oval for the tail. Add two connecting lines to the body. Draw four small triangles to these lines for the back fins. Add a larger crescent to the front of the oval for the snout. Then, add two large triangles to the oval for the front fins.

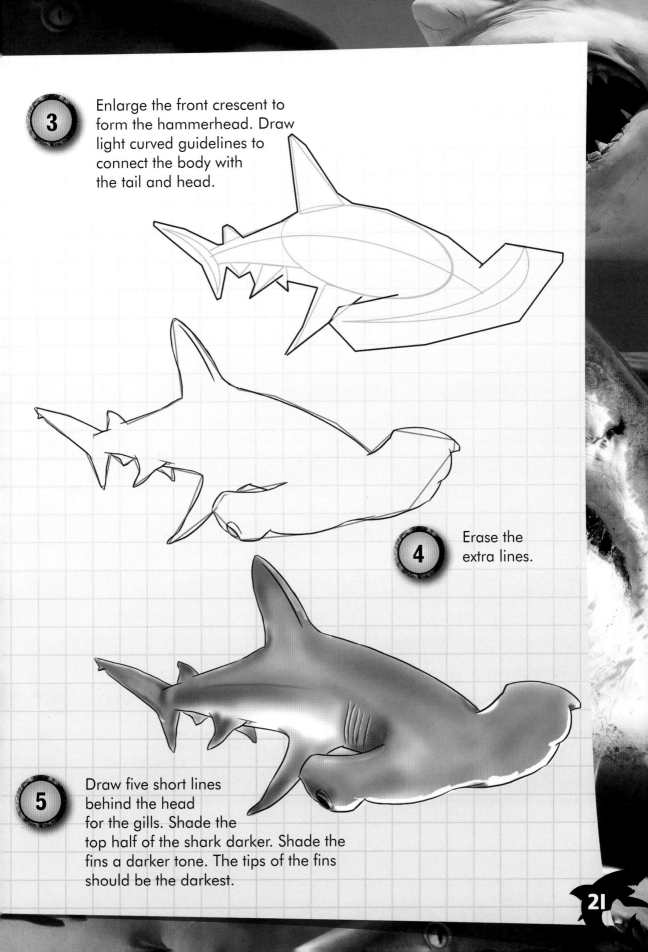

3 Enlarge the front crescent to form the hammerhead. Draw light curved guidelines to connect the body with the tail and head.

4 Erase the extra lines.

5 Draw five short lines behind the head for the gills. Shade the top half of the shark darker. Shade the fins a darker tone. The tips of the fins should be the darkest.

Glossary

camouflage (KAM-uh-flahzh): coloring that makes animals, people, or objects look like their surroundings

carnivore (KAHR-nuh-vohr): an animal that eats other animals

cartilage (KAHR-tuh-lij): a strong, flexible material that forms parts of the body of animals

crevices (KREV-is-iz): cracks or splits in something, such as a rock

dimension (di-MEN-shun): the measurement of length, width, or height

gills (GILZ): parts of a fish that are used for breathing

impulses (IM-puls-iz): sudden forces that causes motion

mollusks (MOL-uhskz): animals with a soft body and no backbone, usually protected by a hard shell

prey (PRAY): an animal that is hunted by another animal for food

predators (PRED-uh-turz): animals that kill other animals for food

proportions (pruh-POHR-shunz): the relations of one thing to another with regard to size

schools (SKUHLZ): groups of fish

shade (SHAYD): to make part of a drawing darker than the rest

skeleton (SKEL-i-tun): the framework of bones that supports and protects the body of an animal with a backbone

snout (SNOUT): the long front part of an animal's head, including the nose, mouth, and jaws

Index

Websites to Visit

www.flmnh.ufl.edu/fish/sharks/sharks.htm
Gives information about sharks, including attacks, sharks on lists of endangered animals, and the history of sharks.

www.pbs.org/wgbh/nova/sharks/
Explores the coast of Costa Rica's Cocos Island, which boasts more sharks than any other place on Earth. Discover different kinds of sharks and their habitats.

www.seaworld.org
Discover all you want to know about sharks: their senses, habitats, diets, and physical characteristics.

About the Author
Gare Thompson has written over 200 children's books. He has also taught elementary school. He lives in Massachusetts with his wife. During the summer, he loves to go to the ocean, but he always watches out for sharks.

About the Illustrator
Vinay Kumar Sharma has illustrated a number of children's books. He has a Masters in Fine Arts. Vinay draws primarily realistic art. He loves drawing the world around him. Vinay lives with his family in New Delhi. He has been working for Q2A Media for three years.

**Indianapolis
Marion County
Public Library**

**Renew by Phone
269-5222**

Renew on the Web
www.imcpl.org

For General Library Information
please call 269-1700

DEMCO